Dealing with Challenges

Loneliness

By Meg Gaertner

level
2
little blue
readers

www.littlebluehousebooks.com

Little Blue House is distributed by North Star Editions:
sales@northstareditions.com | 888-417-0195

Produced for Little Blue House by Red Line Editorial.

Photographs ©: Shutterstock Images, cover, 4, 7, 9, 10, 15, 17, 18, 21, 24 (top right), 24 (bottom left), 24 (bottom right); iStockphoto, 13, 23, 24 (top left)

Library of Congress Control Number: 2021916791

ISBN
978-1-64619-486-5 (hardcover)
978-1-64619-513-8 (paperback)
978-1-64619-565-7 (ebook pdf)
978-1-64619-540-4 (hosted ebook)

Printed in the United States of America
Mankato, MN
012022

About the Author

Meg Gaertner enjoys reading, writing, dancing, and being outside. She lives in Minnesota.

Table of Contents

Loneliness

A girl is at a new school.

She does not know who to sit with
at lunch.

She feels lonely.

A boy's friends are on vacation.

He has no one to play with.

He feels lonely.

It hurts to feel lonely.

But there are ways to feel better.

team

Making Friends

Join a club or sports team.

You can make new friends that way.

It might be scary to meet

new people.

Start by saying hi.

Share something about yourself.

Or ask your new

friends questions.

friends

Invite your new friends to play with you.

Or ask if you can join their fun.

Being Alone

Sometimes other people are not around.

But being alone doesn't mean being lonely.

You can play by yourself.

You can draw a picture.

You can even make up a
silly dance.
You can have fun on your own!

dance

Glossary

dance

picture

friends

team

Index